HEADLINES FROM HISTORY™

The Assault on Fort Wagner

Black Soldiers Make a Stand in South Carolina Battle

Wendy Vierow

The Rosen Publishing Group's
PowerKids Press™
New York

For Carl

Published in 2004 by The Rosen Publishing Group, Inc.
29 East 21st Street, New York, NY 10010

First Edition

Editor: Frances E. Ruffin

Book Design: Michael de Guzman

Photo Credits: Cover (inset photo), p. 15 Hulton/Archive/Getty Images; cover (rifle) Photo by Peter Latner, Minnesota Historical Society; cover (hats) Cindy Reiman; pp. 5, 9 Library of Congress, Prints and Photographs Division; p. 6 courtesy of the South Carolina Historical Society; p. 7 Irma and Paul Milstein Division of United States History, Local History and Genealogy, The New York Public Library, Astor, Lenox and Tilden Foundations; p. 11 Print Collection, Miriam and Ira D. Wallach Division of Art, Prints and Photographs, The New York Public Library, Astor, Lenox and Tilden Foundations; p. 12 Boston Athenaeum; pp. 16, 17 courtesy of the Moorland-Spingarn Research Center, Howard University; p. 19 courtesy of the Ohio Historical Society; p. 21 © CORBIS.

Vierow, Wendy.
The assault on Fort Wagner : Black Union soldiers make a stand in South Carolina battle / Wendy Vierow.
p. cm. — (Headlines from history)
Includes bibliographical references and index.
Summary: Provides an overview of the role of African American soldiers in the Civil War, focusing on the establishment of the 54th Massachusetts Regiment and their role in the attack on Fort Wagner on Morris Island, South Carolina.
ISBN 0-8239-6223-7
1. Morris Island (S.C.), Battle of, 1863—Juvenile literature. 2. Fort Wagner (S.C.)—History—Juvenile literature. 3. United States. Army. Massachusetts Infantry Regiment, 54th (1863–1865)—Juvenile literature. 4. United States—History—Civil War, 1861–1865—Participation, African American—Juvenile literature. 5. Charleston (S.C.)—History—Civil War, 1861–1865—Juvenile literature. [1. United States—History—Civil War, 1861–1865—Participation, African American. 2. Morris Island (S.C.), Battle of, 1863. 3. Fort Wagner (S.C.) 4. United States. Army. Massachusetts Infantry Regiment, 54th (1863–1865)] I. Title. II. Series.
E475.63 .V54 2003
973.7'34—dc21

2001007246

Manufactured in the United States of America

CONTENTS

The United States Enters a Civil War

People can no longer see Fort Wagner in Charleston, South Carolina. It was washed away by the Atlantic Ocean years ago. However, during the **Civil War**, Fort Wagner was the site of an important battle. The Civil War began in Charleston, South Carolina, on April 12, 1861, when Southern soldiers fired on U.S. troops at Fort Sumter. The main reason for the war was a disagreement between Northerners and Southerners over **slavery**. Slaves had no rights. Many Northerners thought that slavery was wrong. Many Southerners said that they needed the free labor of slaves to run plantations, or large farms.

This print shows the battle at Fort Sumter in South Carolina that started the Civil War.

By 1861, leaders of Southern states decided that their states should break away from the United States. They formed their own country, called the **Confederate States of America**. They elected former Mississippi senator Jefferson Davis as president of the Confederacy. Abraham Lincoln was president of the United States.

Confederates Build Fort Wagner

From the beginning of the Civil War, U.S. forces, known as **Union** forces, wanted to capture the city of Charleston, South Carolina. Charleston was an important port for the South. Ships brought goods into and out of Charleston. If the Union could capture the port of Charleston, the Confederacy would have fewer supplies to use in the war. However, many forts guarded Charleston Harbor.

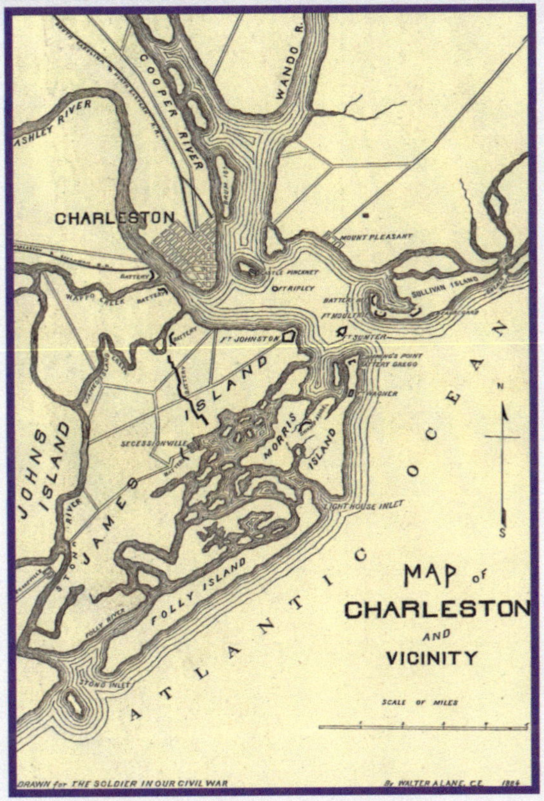

This map shows Charleston Harbor, an important port for the Confederacy.

In June 1862, Union forces tried to capture Charleston but did not succeed. After this Union defeat, **Confederates** built Fort Wagner on Morris Island near Charleston. It was built to make Charleston safer against another Union attack. Fort Wagner was made of wood and thick, sand walls. The thick walls protected Confederate soldiers at the fort from Union gunshots. Confederates armed Fort Wagner with more than a dozen cannons. The cannons could shoot at Union soldiers who tried to attack the fort.

Soldiers of the Union army in Fort Wagner in 1863 built bombproof shelters that protected them against attack from Confederate soldiers.

African Americans Join the Union Army

When the Civil War started in 1861, many African American men wanted to join the Union army. However, this was against the law. Although most white Northerners were against slavery, they were still **prejudiced** against African Americans. They thought that African American men could not fight as well as white men.

As the war continued, many people grew tired of it. Many white men did not want to fight anymore. Union leaders needed new soldiers. In July 1862, Congress passed laws to let African American men join the Union army. Two months

The African American soldiers in this 1865 photograph belonged to the U.S. 107th Colored Infantry of Arlington, Virginia.

later, President Lincoln issued the **Emancipation Proclamation**. This proclamation stated that slaves in states fighting against the United States would be freed on January 1, 1863. The proclamation did not actually free any slaves, because the Confederacy didn't accept it. However, the proclamation encouraged many African American men to join the Union army.

African Americans Become Union Soldiers

African American soldiers joined the Union army to fight. Many Union officers, however, ordered African American soldiers to dig ditches and build roads. These officers thought that only white soldiers should fight, although other officers disagreed with them. Even though Union officers were against slavery, they did not treat African Americans equally. The Union army **segregated** black soldiers from white soldiers. Union leaders chose white officers to lead most African American soldiers. Only a few African American officers were selected as leaders.

Frederick Douglass, who was once a slave, believed that it was important for African American men to become soldiers.

Then no one could deny that they were citizens. Douglass was a famous speaker and an **abolitionist** who was against slavery. He said, "Once let the black man get upon his person the brass letters 'U.S.,' let him get an eagle on his buttons and a **musket** on his shoulder and bullets in his pocket, and there is no power on earth which can deny that he has earned the right to citizenship in the United States."

Abolitionist Frederick Douglass worked during his lifetime to remind the nation that black people were Americans, too.

The 54th Massachusetts Regiment Is Formed

In February 1863, the governor of Massachusetts organized a **regiment** of African American **volunteers**. It was called the 54th Regiment of Massachusetts Volunteer **Infantry**. The 54th was the first African American regiment in a free state. The governor asked Captain Robert Gould Shaw, a white man and the son of

abolitionists, to lead the regiment. Accepting the position took courage on Shaw's part. He would face **discrimination** from whites if he chose to work alongside African Americans. Shaw accepted the job. He became a colonel in the Union army in May 1863.

African Americans, including Frederick Douglass's sons, Lewis and Charles, came from many states to join the 54th. Soldiers of the 54th were paid $10 a month, $3 less than white soldiers were paid. Shaw and his entire regiment, including white officers, refused to accept their pay until Shaw's soldiers were paid the same as white soldiers. The law for equal pay was not changed until June 15, 1864.

This photograph shows Colonel Robert Gould Shaw, commander of the 54th Regiment of Massachusetts Volunteer Infantry.

The Union Attacks Fort Wagner

In July 1863, Colonel Shaw's commander asked him to lead 600 members of the 54th Massachusetts in an attack on Fort Wagner. The 54th would lead the attack against the fort. They would be followed by eight units of white soldiers. General Quincy Gillmore was in charge of Union forces. General Pierre Gustave Toutant Beauregard was in charge of Confederate forces.

The charge was very dangerous. The men of the 54th had little experience in battle. They had never attacked a fort before. On July 18, 1863, the 54th began their attack, running across a narrow beach to the fort. Confederates fired on the

This Currier and Ives print shows Colonel Shaw and the men of the 54th Massachusetts storming a hill at Fort Wagner.

54th. Finally the 54th reached the fort. Soon afterward Shaw was killed at the fort.

Also killed in the fight was the Union soldier carrying the U.S. flag. Union sergeant William Carney, an African American, took the flag and planted it on the fort. For a brief time, the Union had control of Fort Wagner.

The Union Retreats

The 54th fought bravely against Confederate forces at Fort Wagner. Both of Frederick Douglass's sons survived the attack. Later, Lewis Douglass wrote, "Men fell all around me. A [cannon] shell would explode and clear a space of twenty feet [6 m], our men would close up again, but it was no use; we had to retreat, which was a very hazardous undertaking. How I got out of the fight alive I cannot tell, but I am here."

Lewis Douglass, a son of Frederick Douglass, was a sergeant-major in the Union army.

After about an hour of fighting, Confederate forces forced the 54th to abandon the fort. Sergeant William Carney held the U.S. flag during the retreat. Although he was badly wounded, with injuries to his head, chest, arm, and leg, Carney carried the flag back to safety. Other units of the Union army continued to fight but could not capture the fort. The Confederates won the battle.

Charles Douglass, another son of Frederick Douglass, served with the 54th Massachusetts alongside his brother Lewis. Both men survived the attack on Fort Wagner.

Northerners Support African American Soldiers

Although the 54th Massachusetts lost the fight at Fort Wagner in August 1863, it was an important event. The African American soldiers of the 54th had shown that they could fight well. In a July 1863 diary entry, Charlotte Forten, an African American teacher, wrote, "The 54th . . . fought bravely!"

The events at Fort Wagner convinced many Union generals that African Americans could fight with courage. In August Union general Ulysses S. Grant wrote to President Lincoln, "They will make good soldiers. . . ."

Magazines and newspapers praised the men of the 54th for

The article on the opposite page appeared in the Cleveland Gazette *newspaper on May 10, 1866.*

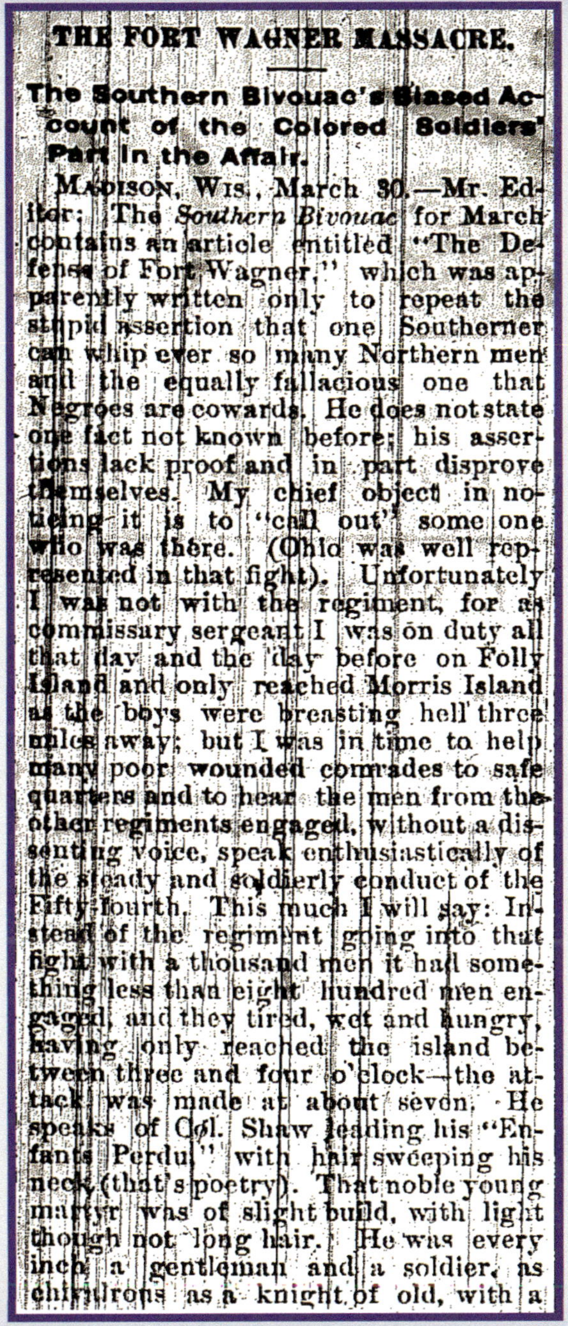

THE FORT WAGNER MASSACRE.

The Southern Bivouac's Biased Account of the Colored Soldiers' Part in the Affair.

MADISON, WIS., March 30.—Mr. Editor: The *Southern Bivouac* for March contains an article entitled "The Defense of Fort Wagner," which was apparently written only to repeat the stupid assertion that one Southerner can whip ever so many Northern men and the equally fallacious one that Negroes are cowards. He does not state one fact not known before; his assertions lack proof and in part disprove themselves. My chief object in noticing it is to "call out" some one who was there. (Ohio was well represented in that fight). Unfortunately I was not with the regiment, for as commissary sergeant I was on duty all that day and the day before on Folly Island and only reached Morris Island as the boys were breasting hell three miles away; but I was in time to help many poor wounded comrades to safe quarters and to hear the men from the other regiments engaged, without a dissenting voice, speak enthusiastically of the steady and soldierly conduct of the Fifty-fourth. This much I will say: Instead of the regiment going into that fight with a thousand men it had something less than eight hundred men engaged, and they tired, wet and hungry, having only reached the island between three and four o'clock—the attack was made at about seven. He speaks of Col. Shaw leading his "Enfants Perdu" with hair sweeping his neck (that's poetry). That noble young martyr was of slight build, with light though not long hair. He was every inch a gentleman and a soldier, as chivalrous as a knight of old, with a

their bravery. They helped change the opinions of many Northerners. The *Atlantic Monthly* magazine stated, "Through the cannon smoke of that dark night . . . the colored race shines before many eyes that would not see."

After Fort Wagner, many African Americans joined the Union army. By 1865, 10 percent of all Union soldiers were African Americans.

The Union Captures Fort Wagner

Although the 54th Massachusetts failed to capture Fort Wagner on Morris Island for the Union, General Quincy Gillmore had another plan. He asked members of the 54th and other Union soldiers to dig **trenches** near the fort. The Union army put guns in the trenches. For two months, Union troops fired at Fort Wagner.

Finally on September 6, 1863, Confederate troops left Morris Island. Union troops moved in to use the island as a base. From there, they fired shells at Confederates in Charleston Harbor. The Confederate forces left Charleston in February 1865.

Members of the 54th Massachusetts continued to serve in the

Soldiers camping on Morris Island often clustered their tents near the beach for its cool ocean breezes.

Charleston area for most of the war. They also fought in other places in South Carolina and Florida. After the Union won the war in 1865, the 54th Massachusetts was **discharged**. African American soldiers had proven that they could fight well.

A Soldier from the 54th Receives an Award

In 1900, 37 years after the assault on Fort Wagner, the U.S. government awarded the Medal of Honor to Sergeant William Carney for his bravery at Fort Wagner. He was the first African American to receive this award. Carney, a former slave who had hoped to become a minister, had joined the 54th Massachusetts and had soon become a sergeant in the U.S. Army. Carney was honored because he had saved the U.S. flag though he had been seriously wounded. During the battle, a soldier from New York had offered to take the flag from Carney, but Carney had said, "No one but a member of the 54th should carry the colors." Carney had been injured but had continued to carry the U.S. flag, a symbol of freedom.

GLOSSARY

abolitionist (a-buh-LIH-shun-ist) Someone who worked to end slavery.
Civil War (SIH-vul WOR) The war fought between the Northern and Southern states of America from 1861 to 1865.
Confederates (kun-FEH-duh-rets) People who fought for the South during the Civil War.
Confederate States of America (kun-FEH-duh-ret STAYTZ UV uh-MER-ih-kuh) A group of 11 Southern states that declared themselves separate from the United States in 1861.
discharged (dis-CHARJD) To have dismissed, for example, for military service.
discrimination (dis-krih-muh-NAY-shun) Treating a person badly or unfairly just because he or she is different.
Emancipation Proclamation (ih-man-sih-PAY-shun prah-kluh-MAY-shun) The document issued by Abraham Lincoln in 1862 that said slaves in rebelling states were free.
infantry (IN-fun-tree) The part of an army that walks while fighting.
musket (MUS-kit) A gun with a long barrel, which is the part of the gun that looks like a tube.
prejudiced (PREH-juh-disd) To have an unfair opinion about someone based on that person's race, religion, or another quality.
regiment (REH-jih-ment) A military group.
segregated (SEH-gruh-gayted) To have kept people or things apart from the main group.
slavery (SLAY-vuh-ree) The system of one person "owning" another.
trenches (TREN-chez) Long, narrow ditches of earth used to protect soldiers during battles.
Union (YOON-yun) The Northern states during the Civil War.
volunteers (vah-luhn-TEERZ) People who offer to join the army without being asked.

INDEX

PRIMARY SOURCES

Cover: *The Gallant Charge of the Fifty-Fourth Massachusetts*. Print by Currier & Ives (c.1863). From Hulton Archive. **Page 5**: *Bombardment of Fort Sumter, Charleston Harbor: 12th–13th of April, 1861*. Print by Currier & Ives. **Page 6**: Photograph of a bombproof shelter at Fort Wagner. (1863). South Carolina Historical Society. **Page 7**: Map of Charleston, South Carolina and Vicinity c. 1863. From *The soldier in our civil war: a pictorial history of the conflict*. (1884). **Page 9**: *Band of 107th U.S. Colored Infantry*. Photographer, William Morris Smith (1865). Library of Congress. **Page 11**: Frederick Douglass. New York Public Library, Print Collection, Douglass Portrait File. **Page 12**: Portrait of Robert Gould Shaw. Boston Athenaeum. **Page 15**: *The Gallant Charge of the Fifty-Fourth Massachusetts*.(See cover information). **Page 16**: Sergeant-Major Lewis Douglass (1863). Moorland-Spingarn Research Center, Howard University. **Page 17**: Charles Douglass (1863). Moorland-Spingarn Research Center, Howard University. **Page 19**: Fort Wagner Massacre. Newspaper clipping from the *Cleveland Gazette* (May 10, 1886). **Page 21**: Camp of the 9th Maine Infantry on Morris Island during the siege of Charleston. (1863).

WEB SITES

Due to the changing nature of Internet links, PowerKids Press has developed an online list of Web sites related to the subject of this book. This site is updated regularly. Please use this link to access the list: www.powerkidslinks.com/hfh/asltfw/